POCKET RETREAT

from

A JESUS BREVIARY

meditation rendering by
Stephen Joseph Wolf

idjc.org

A QUESTION FOR BEGINNING A RETREAT:

Lord, how do you want me to spend / pray / waste time alone with you?

Pocket Retreat from *A Jesus Breviary*
Copyright © 2023 Stephen Joseph Wolf
All rights reserved.
No part of this book may be copied or reproduced in any form or by any means without the written permission of the publisher, except for the inclusion of brief quotations in a review.

→ This short retreat is drawn from the eight sets of 31 scripture passages in *A Jesus Breviary* offered for meditation on the Jesus story. →

ISBN 978-1-937081-63-8

Stephen Joseph Wolf is retired, a former parish priest (22 lents & holy weeks), spiritual director and retreat leader, and before that a certified public accountant (14 tax seasons), who before that worked as a landscaper, desk clerk, laundry worker, janitor, paper boy, and student, growing up the second of eight sons of a parish secretary and Nashville's best television repairman. He completed a B.S. at MTSU, an M.B.A. at Belmont University, and an M.Div. at Mundelein Seminary.

He continues to write poems and songs and paint folk art icons, sing baritone for the LGBTQ+ chorus *Nashville in Harmony*, play the ukulele with *Music for Seniors* and others, volunteer as a bookkeeper for two non-profits, serve on the board of *PFLAG Nashville*, and gather with the LGBTQ+Catholic group *Always God's Children*. He lives in Nashville with his husband Billy.

www.idjc.org

A JESUS BREVIARY

1st - 31 days of God's Love-Call
These passages are all from the Hebrew Bible, to help sit with God saying "I love you" for as long as we can stand it. If a new awareness of sin surfaces, be not afraid.

2nd - 31 days of Jesus Incarnate
That God would enter human history as one like us in all things but sin was unexpected and laughed at when preached, the surprise of the Word made flesh.

3rd - 31 days of Jesus Miracles
The Son of God shows forth the divine dynamic power in signs opening mind, heart, soul, and strength.

4th - 31 days of Jesus Parables
Which parable leaves you most perplexed? You will want to waste a lot of time with it. Which one seems clear-cut? That one too, until you are perplexed again.

5th - 31 days of Jesus Sayings
These are in Sunday gospel readings in the 3 year cycle.

6th - 31 days of Jesus' Paschal Mystery
The full gift of the self of Jesus in his scandalous cross shows through his death and resurrection to Easter joy.

7th - 31 days of the Holy Spirit
Jesus told us that *the Holy Spirit, the Paraclete, will teach us all things* (John 14:26), the Holy Breath of God.

8th - 31 days on the Christian Life
These timeless readings from the letters attributed to Saints Peter, Paul, James, and John are selected from Morning and Evening Prayer in the *Liturgy of the Hours*.

A Jesus Breviary © 2015 Stephen Joseph Wolf
ISBN 978-1-937081-40-9   Ebook ISBN 978-1-937081-41-6

1st
GOD's LOVE-CALL

What do you hear when you read God's word in the Bible? I hear a very long love letter. The Bible as a whole can be read in this simple message from God:

I made you, I know you, and I love you.

This can be a message of great consolation. If I am aware of not living as if God loves me, it can nudge as a challenge, not to be better to earn God's love, but a reminder of my desire to live a fidelity-response to God's complete love for me.

It has been an honor to journey with many good folks in the *Spiritual Exercises* of St. Ignatius of Loyola in At-Home Retreats and in spiritual direction. The first part of the exercises is to sit with intention in the reality of God's provision and love. This means letting God say and repeat, *I love you*. The passages listed can help let this message sink into one's being. Though most of them are psalms and canticles to sing to God, as scripture they are also meant to be read as part of God's revelation; so whether the words are addressed to God, to someone else, or to the reader, we can hear them as God's love letter to us.

If you feel drawn to a word or phrase or image, be open to the possibility that the Holy Spirit has something to say in it, and consider letting that be your word to breathe through the day.

*My Beloved,
I have made you in my image,
one and unique,
not like anyone ever has been
or ever will be made in my image.*

*Having made you,
I know you,
all the great things
your ego wants everyone to know,
those things
you do not want anyone to know,
and everything
you do not yet know yourself.*

*And in knowing you,
I love you,
neither because of your strengths
nor in spite of your weaknesses;
there is nothing you can do
that will make me love you,
and there is nothing you can do
that will keep me from loving you.*

*Remember this always:
that I love you just is.*

- God

LECTIO DIVINA
lek'-see-oh div-ee'-nuh

The ancient way (from the monks and nuns) of listening to God in *lectio divina* can be as simple as choosing a word or phrase or image from the passage, sitting with it perhaps without thinking about it, and breathing to listen.

When you have decided how much time you will be with the Lord in prayer, here are the traditional four parts to it, but keep it simple.

1. *Lectio* (read)

Read the passage of the word of God with attention, silently, aloud, or in a whisper. If drawn to a word or phrase or image, stop.

2. *Meditatio* (ponder)

Breathe. Repeat the word or phrase or image over and over as you breathe. Let it sink into your mind, heart, soul and strength. Savor the word. Ask just one question: *Why this? What do you wish to say, Lord?*

3. *Oratio* (pray)

Be not afraid to enter into a spontaneous and loving dialogue with God. Talk to God as you would talk to your closest most intimate friend. Be totally honest about what you are thinking and feeling. Are any memories provoked? What do you want to say to God who loves you just the way you are?

You may be drawn to praise, thanksgiving, contrition, petition, desires, decisions, resolutions, commitments, dedications… God is interested in everything you have to say and will not judge you. You get to decide whether you will integrate this Word of God into your heart, life and work, or whether you will reject it or dismiss it as of no worth or value to you.

4. *Contemplatio* (let go)

For the remainder of the time you have set aside, go back to the word, phrase or image. Breathe. Relax. Simply repeat the word, phrase or image over and over. When distracting thoughts or feelings enter your mind (they will), go back to your word. There is nothing to accomplish; just give this time to the God who loves you. Sitting in God's presence in this silence, you are making an act of faith that God is working in you in God's own time and way.

When your time is up, offer a prayer of gratitude. Many people who do *Lectio Divina* find regular journaling to be helpful.

This summary of **Lectio Divina** comes from many guides, all of whom have my deep gratitude, especially Rev. Paul Wachdorf of Chicago's Mundelein Seminary.

GOD'S LOVE-CALL

God's Love
for you and for me is complete,
and our God is calling us.

Each person is created
to praise, revere, and serve our Lord God,
and in this vocation
to find salvation in eternal life.

The other things on the face of the earth
are created for us all, to help each person
find and fulfill the *purpose/reason/end/…*
for which he or she is created.

We humans are to use well the other things
to the extent they help us discover and fulfill
our *purpose/reason/end/…*

Sooner or later each of us
will need to rid ourselves of the other things
that get in the way of this personal vocation.

It will come to be our desire
to be indifferent to all created things,
as far as we are allowed free choice
and consistent with faithful commitments
already freely made.

And so, our concern will be to see
all good things in unbiased balance,
and we will not prefer
health to sickness,
riches to poverty,
the world's honor to its dishonor,
or a long life to a short life,
and this balance of indifference
will hold for all other things.

When my one desire comes to be
whatever is more conducive
to the *purpose/reason/end/...*
for which I am created,
may my choices reflect that desire.
If not now, when?

The Principle and Foundation
of St. Ignatius of Loyola, d. 1556
is usually part of the first days of
*The Spiritual Exercises (*para. 23).

GOD'S LOVE-CALL
1

God, you are my God;
you I earnestly seek.
My soul, she thirsts for you,
my body, he longs for you,
as in a land with no water,
dry and weary.
So in the sanctuary I saw you,
beheld you in your power and glory.
Your love is better than life itself;
my lips will glorify you.
So I will praise you
in all the ways I am alive;
in your name I will lift up my hands.
As with fatness and richness,
my soul will be satisfied;
with singing lips
my mouth will sing praise.
When I remember you on my bed,
through night watches I think of you,
you who are my help;
then in the shadow of your wings I sing.
My very self stays close to you;
your right hand upholds me.

Psalm 63:1-8

31 days of GOD's LOVE-CALL

1	Psalm 63:1-8
2	Psalm 46
3	Isaiah 55:1-13
4	Wisdom of Solomon 9:1-6,9-11
5	Psalm 23
6	Psalm 139:1-18,23-24
7	Isaiah 43:1-5a
8	Exodus 16:4-5,9,10b
9	Hosea 2:10-22
10	Psalm 131
11	Psalm 8
12	Psalm 103
13	Psalm 104
14	Psalm 19
15	1st Kings 19:4-9a,11-13
16	Jeremiah 29:11-14
17	Ezekiel 16:4-13
18	Jeremiah 18:1-6
19	Genesis 2:4-25
20	Genesis 1:24-31
21	Isaiah 54:4-10
22	Deuteronomy 30:15-20
23	Isaiah 62:1-5
24	Ecclesiastes 3:1-11,14b
25	Psalm 62:2-10,12,13a
26	Wisdom of Solomon 11:21-12:1
27	Psalm 91:1-12,14-16
28	Ezekiel 36:24-28
29	Ezekiel 37:1-14
30	Isaiah 40:1-11
31	Psalm 130

2nd
JESUS INCARNATE

Jesus is that man who lived in the first third of what we now call the first century, near the Sea of Galilee in what is now called Israel, who we also know as God, Son of God, Christ the Anointed One, Savior, Redeemer, Risen Lord, and a host of other names.

Incarnate means enfleshed or embodied, or for Christians, the Word become Flesh. This means that God has chosen to enter human history as one of us. Tell a little child that there was a day when Jesus was exactly as tall as he or she is today. Tell a teen that Jesus too lived in his own in-betweenness. Tell a student that Jesus too had to learn. Tell the adult being tempted that so was Jesus, one like us in all things but sin.

Anytime we proclaim his divinity, his God-ness, to the diminishment of his humanity, we may fall into what we call heresy. And anytime we proclaim his humanity to the exclusion of his divinity, we may fall into heresy. For a Christian, Jesus is Son of God and Son of a human being, Mary. He is fully God and fully human, not half God and half man, as a teacher would say, not only God on his Poppa's side and human on his Momma's side, but completely God and completely human. The two natures of the one person of Jesus can be seen in these gospel classics.

Be in the story.
Imagine yourself as a character in the scene.
What do you see, hear, smell, taste and feel?

Lord Jesus,
You are fully God
and fully human.

We your brothers and sisters
are created by God
and begotten of our parents.

Begotten of God and Mary,
you are not a creature;

as Son of God you know me
better than I know myself;

as Son of Mary you entered all of
human history, joy, and sorrow.

As I am made in God's image,
give me the grace necessary
to grow into your likeness,
New 'Adam, Savior,
Brother and Friend.
Amen.

JESUS INCARNATE
7
THE WORD

In the beginning is the Word and the Word is with God, and the Word is God. This one is in the beginning with God. Through him all things become, and without him not one thing which is to be becomes. In him is life, and the life (*zoe*) is the light (*phos*) of all humanity; and the light shines in the night, and the night does not overtake it. There is a human, sent from God, whose name is John. This human comes for witness, that he might witness to the light, that all might believe through him. He is not the light, but a witness to the light. The true light, which enlightens every human, is coming into the cosmos. He is in the cosmos, and the cosmos becomes through him, and the cosmos does not know him... To as many as receive him he gives the right to become children of God, the ones believing in his name, who are born not by blood nor by will of flesh nor by human will, but of God.

And the Word becomes flesh
and tents among us,
and we gaze on his glory,
glory as of an only begotten from a father,
full of grace and truth.

Prologue of the Gospel of **John 1:1-14**

31 days of JESUS INCARNATE

1. ANNUNCIATION — Luke 1:26-38
2. NATIVITY (Christmas) — Luke 2:15-21
3. THE MAJI — Matthew 2:1-12
4. SIMEON & ANNA — Luke 2:22-40
5. RETURN from EXILE in EGYPT — Matthew 2:19-23
6. TWELVE YEARS OLD — Luke 2:41-52
7. THE WORD — Prologue of the Gospel of John 1:1-14
8. BAPTISM — Matthew 3:13-17 Mk 1:9-11 Lk 3:21-22
9. TEMPTATION — Matt 4:1-11 Mark 1:12-13 Luke 4:1-13
10. REJECTION — Luke 4:14-30 Mt 13:54-58 Mk 6:1-6
11. SIMON, ANDREW... — Mark 1:14-20 Mt 4:12-22 Lk 5:1-11
12. DAY in the MINISTRY — Mk 1:29-39 Mt 4:23-25 Lk 4:38-44
13. NICODEMUS at NIGHT — John 3:1-21
14. WOMAN at the WELL — John 4:5-42
15. LEVI is CALLED — Mark 2:13-17 Luke 5:27-32
    In Matthew 9:9-13 the tax-collector's name is Matthew.
16. FIELD of GRAIN — Mark 2:23-28 Mt 12:1-8 Lk 6:1-5
17. THE TWELVE & THE WOMEN — Luke 6:12-19 & 8:1-3
    Matthew 10:1-4 Mark 3:13-19
18. LOVE YOUR ENEMIES — Matthew 5:43-48 Luke 6:27-36
19. THE FAMILY — Mark 3:20-21 John 10:20
    Mark 3:31-35 Matthew 12:46-50 Luke 8:19-21
20. THE BREAD of LIFE — John 6:52-53,60-69
21. DISCIPLES of the BAPTIZER — Luke 7:18-23 Mt 11:2-6
22. ANOINTING by a WOMAN — Luke 7:36-50
23. PROFESSION — Matt 16:13-20 Mk 8:27-33 Lk 9:18-21
24. TRANSFIGURATION — Mk 9:2-10 Mt 17:1-9 Lk 9:28-36
25. WOMAN CAUGHT in ADULTERY — John 8:2-11
26. RICH YOUNG MAN — Mt 19:16-22 Mk 10:17-27 Lk 18:18-30
27. JAMES & JOHN — Mark 10:35-45 Matthew 20:20-28
28. ZACCHAEUS — Luke 19:1-10
29. ENTRY on a DONKEY — Mark 11:1-10
    Matthew 21:1-11; Luke 19:28-40; John 12:12-19
30. CLEANSING the TEMPLE — Mark 11:15b-18
    Matthew 21:12-16 Luke 19:45-48 John 2:13-25
31. AUTHORITY QUESTIONED
    Mark 11:27-33 Matthew 21:23-27 Luke 20:1-8
    Mark 12:28-34 Matthew 22:34-40

3rd
JESUS MIRACLES

Lord Jesus,
in your miraculous ministry
on the face of the earth
from Nazareth and Cana
and Capernaum and Galilee
to the Jordan and in Samaria
and Jericho and Jerusalem
you showed forth with authority
the compassion and power
of the God and Abba of us all.

Transform my ponder-meditation
on these good news stories
into a contemplative gaze on you,
my Physician, Redeemer,
Brother and Friend.
Amen.

JESUS MIRACLES
2
CATCH of FISH

Getting into one of the boats, Simon's, Jesus asks him to put out a little. Sitting he teaches the crowds out of the boat. When he stops speaking, he says to Simon, "Put out into the deep, and let down your nets for a catch."

Simon answers, "Master, laboring through the whole night we took nothing; but at your word I will let down the nets."

Doing this they net a multitude of many fishes, and their nets are being torn. They signal to their partners in the other boat that they should come to help them. They come and fill both boats so that they are sinking.

Seeing, Simon Peter falls at the knees of Jesus saying, "Depart from me, Lord, for I am a sinful human." Astonishment seizes him and all the ones with him at the catch of the fishes they are taking, and likewise James and John, sons of Zebedee, who are partners with Simon.

Jesus says to Simon, "Fear you not; from now on you will catch alive human beings."

Bringing the boats down onto the land and leaving all things, they follow him.

Luke 5:3-11

31 days of JESUS MIRACLES

1. WATER & WINE (1st of 6 or 7 Signs in John)   John 2:1-11
2. CATCH of FISH   Luke 5:3-11
3. SON of a ROYAL OFFICIAL   John 4:46-54
4. DEMONIAC   Mark 1:21-28   Luke 4:31-37
5. LEPER   Matthew 8:1-4   Mark 1:40-45   Luke 5:12-16
6. PARALYTIC   Mark 2:1-12   Matthew 9:1-8   Luke 5:17-26
7. SICK MAN at BETHESDA   John 5:1-17
8. MAN with a WITHERED HAND   Mark 3:1-6
   Matthew 12:9-14   Luke 6:6-11
9. SERVANT of a CENTURIAN   Matthew 8:5-13   Luke 7:1-10
10. SON of a WIDOW   Luke 7:11-17
11. CALMING of a STORM   Matthew 8:23-27
    Mark 4:35-41   Luke 8:22-25
12. GERASENE-GADARENE DEMONIAC   Mark 5:1-20
    Matthew 8:28-34   Luke 8:26-39
13. DAUGHTER of JAIRUS & WOMAN in the CROWD
    Luke 8:40-56   Matthew 9:18-26   Mark 5:21-43
14. TWO BLIND MEN   Mathew 9:27-31
15. POSSESSED MUTE   Matthew 9:32-35
16. FEEDING of FIVE THOUSAND   John 6:1-15
    Matthew 14:13-21   Mark 6:34-44   Luke 9:10-17
17. WALKING on WATER   John 6:16-21
    Mark 6:45-52   Matthew 14:22-33
18. WOMAN of CANAAN   Matthew 15:21-28   Mark 7:24-30
19. DEAF MUTE   Mark 7:31-37
20. FEEDING of FOUR THOUSAND   Mt 15:32-39   Mk 8:1-10
21. BLIND MAN of BETHSAIDA   Mark 8:22-26
22. POSSESSED BOY   Lk 9:37-43a   Mt 17:14-20   Mk 9:14-29
23. PROVISION for TEMPLE TAX   Matthew 17:22-27
24. MAN BORN BLIND   John 9:1-41
25. WOMAN CRIPPLED   Luke 13:10-17
26. MAN with DROPSY   Luke 14:1-6
27. TEN LEPERS   Luke 17:11-19
28. BLIND BARTIMAEUS   Mark 10:46-52
    Matthew 20:29-34   Luke 18:35-43
29. RAISING of LAZARUS   John 11:1-45
30. CURSING of a FIG TREE   Mark 11:12-14,20-25   Mt 21:18-22
31. HEALING of an EAR   Luke 22:47-51

4th
JESUS PARABLES

Lord Jesus,
Master & Teacher,
in your parables
you invite us into listening
with the ear that our Abba
opens in our hearts.

Friendship takes time
as do your parables.

Grace me with patient time
to hear what you teach
and wisdom and courage
to live it and do it.

Transform my ponder-meditation
inside these good news parables
into a contemplative gaze on you,
my Savior, Redeemer,
Brother & Friend.
Amen.

JESUS PARABLES
4
GOOD SAMARITAN

A certain lawyer stands up testing Jesus saying, "Teacher, what do I do to inherit eternal life?"

He says to him, "What has been written in the law? How do you read it?"

He answers,
"You shall love the Lord your God
 with all your heart
 and with all your soul
 and with all your strength
 and with all your mind,
 and your neighbor as yourself."

He says to him,
"Rightly do you answer; do this and you shall live."

But wishing to make himself just he says, "And who is my neighbor?"

Taking him up Jesus says,

"A certain man is going down from Jerusalem to Jericho. He falls in with robbers, who both stripping him and laying blows on him go away leaving him half dead.

By coincidence a certain priest is going down in that way, and seeing him passes by opposite.

Likewise also a Levite, coming upon the place and seeing, passes by opposite.

And a certain Samaritan journeying comes upon him and seeing is filled with pity, and approaching binds up his wounds pouring on oil and wine, and placing him on his own beast brings him to an inn and cares for him.

The next day, he takes out and gives two denarii to the innkeeper and says, 'You care for him and whatever you spend in addition when I return I will repay you.'

Who of these three seems to you to have become neighbor of the one falling into the robbers?"

He says,
"The one doing the mercy with him."

And Jesus says to him,
"Go, and you do likewise."

Luke 10:29-37
Two denarii *is the wage for two days of work.*

31 days of JESUS PARABLES

1. NEW WINE — Mark 2:18-22 Mt 9:16-17 Lk 5:33-39
2. CHILDREN of the MARKETPLACE — Mt 11:12-19 Lk 7:28-35
3. THE SOWER & GOOD EARTH — Mark 4:3-20 Matthew 13:3-23 Luke 8:4-15
4. GOOD SAMARITAN — Luke 10:29-37
5. RICH FOOL — Luke 12:16-21
6. RAVENS & LILIES — Luke 12:22-32 Matthew 6:25-34
7. GRAIN GROWING — Mark 4:26-29
8. MUSTARD SEED — Mark 4:30-32 Mt 13:31-32 Lk 13:18-19
   LEAVEN — Luke 13:20-21 Matthew 13:33
9. WEEDS & WHEAT — Matthew 13:24-30
10. TREASURE & PEARL & NET & HEAD of HOUSEHOLD — Matthew 13:44-52
11. LATRINE — Mark 7:14-23 Mathew 15:10-20
12. VIGILANT SERVANT — Mark 13:32-37 Luke 12:35-40
13. FAITHFUL SERVANT — Matthew 24:45-51 Luke 12:42-48
14. BARREN FIG TREE — Luke 13:6-9
15. MEGA BANQUET — Luke 14:16-24 Mathew 22:1-14
16. FAMILY & TOWER & TROOPS & SALT — Luke 14:26-35 Matthew 5:13, 10:37, 16:24 Mark 8:34-37, 9:49-50
17. ONE LOST SHEEP — Luke 15:1-7 Matthew 18:12-14
    ONE LOST COIN — Luke 15:8-10
18. LOST SON — Luke 15:11-32
19. STEWARD of INJUSTICE — Luke 16:1-13
20. RICH MAN & LAZARUS — Luke 16:19-31
21. UNFORGIVING DEBTOR — Matthew 18:21-35
22. UNPROFITABLE SERVANTS — Luke 17:7-10
23. PERSISTENT WIDOW — Luke 18:1-8
24. WORKERS in the VINEYARD — Matthew 20:1-16
25. PHARISEE & TAX COLLECTOR — Luke 18:9-14
26. TWO SONS — Matthew 21:28-32
27. TENANT FARMERS — Mark 12:1-11 Matthew 21:33-46 Luke 20:9-19
28. TEN VIRGINS — Matthew 25:1-13
29. TALENTS — Matthew 25:14-30 Luke 19:11-27 (mina coins)
30. SHEEP & GOATS & WORKS of MERCY — Matthew 25:31-46
31. VINE & BRANCHES — John 15:1-8

5th
JESUS SAYINGS

Lord Jesus,
your word
helps me look at my life
with neither condemnation
nor complacency;

when I am in trouble
guide me in safe consolation;

when I am proud
wake up a teachable disciple;

and when I am nowhere
draw me to your side,
my Savior, Redeemer,
Brother and Friend.
Amen.

JESUS SAYINGS
8

Allow the children to come to me
and do not prevent them,
for of such is the reign of God.
Mark 10:14

Amen I tell you, whoever
does not receive the reign of God as a child
by no means may enter into it.
Mark 10:15

Go, sell what things you have
and give to the poor
and you will have treasure in heaven,
and come follow me.
Mark 10:21

It is easier
for a camel to go through the eye of a needle
than for one who is rich to enter into
the reign of God.
Mark 10:25

With humans it is impossible
but not with God,
for all things are possible with God.
Mark 10:27

JESUS SAYINGS
17

The reign of heaven is like
a treasure hidden in a field
which a human finds and hides
and in joy goes and sells everything
and buys that field.
Matthew 13:44

The reign of heaven is like
a merchant seeking fine pearls,
who finds one precious pearl
and going away sells everything and buys it.
Matthew 13:45,46

Every scribe discipled to the reign of heaven
is like a head of a household
who puts forth from the treasure
things both new and old.
Matthew 13:52

Take courage; it is me. Come.
Matthew 14:27,29

Little-faith, why did you doubt?
Matthew 14:31

JESUS SAYINGS
20

Put out into the deep
and let down your nets for a catch.
Luke 5:4

I have come to call not the righteous
but sinners to conversion.
Luke 5:32

Blessed are you poor
for yours is the reign of God.
Luke 6:20b

Blessed are you hungering now
for you will be satisfied.
Luke 6:21a

Blessed are you weeping now
for you will laugh.
Luke 6:21b

Blessed are you when humans hate you
and exclude you and reproach you
and kick out your name as dung
for the sake of the Son of humanity.
Luke 6:22

JESUS SAYINGS
30

As I, the Lord and Teacher, washed your feet,
so also are you to wash the feet of each other.
John 13:14

Do not let your hearts be troubled…
I am the way and the truth and the life.
John 14:1,6a

Anyone who loves me will keep my word;
my Abba will love that one within whom
we will come to make our dwelling.
John 14:23

The Holy Spirit, the Paraclete,
will teach you all things.
John 14:26

I am the true vine and my Abba is the grower.
John 15:1

Love one another as I have loved you.
…I have called you friends.
John 15:12,15b

I have much more to tell you
but you cannot bear it yet.
John 16:12

31 days of JESUS SAYINGS

1. TEMPLE BAPTISM   TEMPTATION — Luke & Matthew
2. CALL of ANDREW   FIRST SIGN GOSPEL — John & Mark
3. NAZARETH REJECTION   CALLING — Luke & Matthew
4. WILLING TAKE YOUR MAT   NEW WINE — Mark
5. SABBATH   HOUSE DIVIDED   KINGDOM of GOD — Mark
6. TALITHA KOUM   EPHPHATHA — Mark
7. WHO DO PEOPLE SAY I AM — Mark
8. ALLOW the CHILDREN to COME to ME — Mark
9. NO COMMANDMENT GREATER — Mark
10. SERMON on the MOUNT   BEATITUDES — Matthew
11. SERMON on the MOUNT — Matthew
12. SERMON on the MOUNT — Matthew
13. SERMON on the MOUNT — Matthew
14. BE NOT AFRAID — Matthew
15. COME TO ME   MY YOKE IS GENTLE — Matthew
16. THE KINGDOM of HEAVEN — Matthew
17. THE KINGDOM of HEAVEN — Matthew
18. WHERE TWO or THREE   FORGIVE — Matthew
19. CORPORAL WORKS of MERCY — Matthew
20. SERMON on the PLAIN   BEATITUDES — Luke
21. SERMON on the PLAIN   YOUNG MAN ARISE — Luke
22. FOXES HAVE HOLES and BIRDS HAVE NESTS — Luke
23. ASK SEEK KNOCK — Luke
24. TAKE the LOWEST PLACE   DETACH — Luke
25. GOD, BE MERCIFUL to ME, a SINNER — Luke
26. To SEEK and to SAVE the LOST — Luke
27. GOD SO LOVED the COSMOS — John
28. FIRST to THROW a STONE — John
29. I CAME that THEY MIGHT HAVE LIFE — John
30. The WAY and the TRUTH and the LIFE — John
31. RECEIVE the HOLY SPIRIT — John
       GO into ALL the COSMOS — Mark
       BEHOLD, I AM WITH YOU ALWAYS — Matthew

6th
PASCHAL MYSTERY of JESUS

Lord Jesus Christ,
Son of the Living God
and Paschal Lamb,
In your Passover offering
you made the perfect gift of love,
and through the Easter Mystery
of your victory over death
you call us into eternal life.

The Christian greeting,
"He is Risen!"
overwhelms
the scandal of the cross.

Transform my ponder-meditation
inside these good news mysteries
into a contemplative gaze on you,
my Savior, Redeemer,
Brother and Friend.
Amen.

PASCHAL MYSTERY
3
THE LAST SUPPER

As they eat,
taking a loaf,
   blessing,
   he breaks
   and gives to them
      and says,
      "You take;
         this is my body."

Taking a cup,
   giving thanks,
   he gives to them,
   and all drink of it
      and he says to them,
      "This is my blood of the covenant
         being poured out for many.
            Amen I tell you,
            no more will I drink
            of the fruit of the vine
            until that day when I drink new
            in the reign of God."
Having sung a hymn
they go forth to the Mount of Olives.

Mark 14:22-26 Matthew 26:26-30 Luke 22:14-20

PASCHAL MYSTERY
22
APPEARANCE to MARY of MAGDALA

Mary stands outside the tomb weeping. As she is weeping, she bends into the tomb and behold: two angels in white, sitting, one at the head and one at the feet where the body of Jesus lay.

Those say to her, "Woman, why do you weep?"

She says to them, "They took my Lord, and I do not know where they put him." Saying these things, she turns around, and behold: Jesus standing. She does not know it is Jesus.

Jesus says to her, "Woman, why do you weep? Whom do you seek?"

Thinking that it is the gardener, she says to him, "Sir, if you did carry him, tell me where you put him, and I will take him."

Jesus says to her, "Mary." Turning, she says to him in Hebrew, "Rabboni," meaning "Teacher."

Jesus says to her, "Do not hold on to me, for I have not yet ascended to the Abba. Go to my brothers and sisters and tell them, 'I ascend to my Abba and your Abba, my God and your God.'"

Mary the Magdalene comes announcing to the disciples, "I have seen the Lord," and these things he said to her.

John 20:11-18 Mark 16:9-11

31 days of the PASCHAL MYSTERY of JESUS

1. MANY OTHER THINGS — John 20:30-31 & 21:25
2. ANOINTING at BETHANY — Mark 14:3-9   Matt 26:6-13
3. THE LAST SUPPER — Mark 14:22-26 Mt 26:26-30 Lk 22:14-20
4. FOOT WASHING — John 13:1-17
5. LAST SUPPER DISCOURSE — John 13:31-14:12   Lk 22:24-30
6. AGONY in the GARDEN — Mk 14:32f Mt 26:33f Lk 22:39f
7. BETRAYAL & ARREST — Luke 22:47-53
   Matthew 26:47-56   Mark 14:43-52   John 18:1-11
8. SANHEDRIN — Mk 14:53-64 Mt 26:57-68 Lk 22:54 Jn 18:12-14
9. PETER'S DENIAL — Luke 22:55-62
   Matthew 26:69-75   Mark 14:66-72   John 18:15-18,25-27
10. DEATH of JUDAS — Matthew 27:3-10   Acts 1:16-20
11. PILATE'S QUESTIONS — Luke 23:1-5
    Matthew 27:11-14   Mark 15:2-5   John 18:33-38a; 19:7-11
12. MOCKERY — Luke 22:63-65 & 23:6-12
    John 18:38-19:6   Mark 15:16-20   Matthew 27:27-31a
13. SENTENCE of DEATH — John 19:7-11a,12-16a
    Matthew 27:15-26   Mark 15:6-15   Luke 23:13-25
14. WAY of the CROSS — Lk 23:26-32 Mt 27:31f Mk 15:21 Jn 19:16bf
15. CRUCIFIXION — John 19:19-27
    Matthew 27:33-44   Mark 15:22-32   Luke 23:33-43
16. DEATH of JESUS — Mark 15:33f Mt 27:49f Lk 23:44f Jn 19:28f
17. BURIAL & GUARD — Mt 27:57f Mk 15:42f Lk 23:50f Jn 19:38f
18. THE EMPTY TOMB — Mark 16:1-8
19. THE EMPTY TOMB — Luke 24:1-12
20. THE EMPTY TOMB — John 20:1-10
21. THE EMPTY TOMB — Matthew 28:1-10
22. APPEARANCE to MARY of MAGDALA — John 20:11-18   Mark 16:9-11
23. On the ROAD to EMMAUS — Luke 24:13-35   Mk 16:12-13
24. HIS HANDS & HIS FEET — Luke 24:35-45   Mark 16:14
25. UPPER ROOM — John 20:19-23
26. THOMAS on the EIGHTH DAY — John 20:24-29
27. REPORT of the GUARDS — Matthew 28:11-15
28. APPEARANCE to SEVEN in GALILEE — John 21:1-14
29. BREAKFAST LOVE QUESTION — John 21:15-19
30. COMMISSION — Matthew 28:16-20
31. ASCENSION — Luke 24:46-53   Mark 16:14-20

7th
The HOLY SPIRIT

Come, Holy Spirit,
take hold of my life
and sign me with your holy love;
give me your gifts,
confirm me in faith,
Spirit, Come.

Adapted from a song attributed to
Serafina Di Giacoma

Text: Rabanus Mauras, d. 856, *Veni Creator Spiritus*,
with assistance from the literal translation
© 2008 by Bard Suverkrop-IPA Source, LLC
Music: VENI CREATOR SPIRITUS, LM; Mode VIII

Come/, **Cre**\-a-**tor**\ **Spir**/-**it**,
Souls\ of yours, now\ vis/-it:
Fill/ with grace\ be\-yond/ na/-ture
All/ these hearts\ that you have cre-a\-ted.

You/ are\ named Com-fort-Par-a-clete,
The high-est gift of our giv-ing God,
Font/ of life and fire and lov-ing char-i-ty,
Font/ of spir-it-u-al a\-noin\-ting.

You/ sev\-en-fold\ ho-ly gift,
Fing-er of the right\ hand of God,
You who were prom-ised du-ly by the Ab/-ba,
En-rich our throats\ to speak words\ you want heard.

Kin-dle light in our minds, your ho-ly light,
Send and in-fuse in-to hearts your love.
Hu-man weak-ness dwell-ing in hu-man bod/-ies
Your pow-er streng-thens in-to per-pe-tu-i-ty.

Spir-it, drive a-way ev-'ry en-mit-y
Bring-ing the peace ev-er-last/-ing.
With you, our faith-ful lead-er pro/-ceed/-ing
May we a-void\ all harm/ and e\-vil.

Glo-ry be to God/ the Ab/-ba,
To the Son Res-u\-rec/-ted,
And to the **Ho**-**ly Spir**-**it**, Com-fort-Par-a-clete,
For gen-er-a-tions and each gen-er-a\-tion.

A/\-men/.

HOLY SPIRIT
12
HOW MUCH MORE

And Jesus says to them, "Who of you have a friend to whom you might go at midnight and say, 'Friend, lend me three loaves, for a friend has arrived to me off a journey and I have nothing to set before him.' and that one within answering may say, 'Cause me no trouble; the door has been shut and my children are with me in the bed, so I cannot rise up to give to you.' I tell you, even if he will not rise to give because he is a friend, yet because of persistence, rising he will give as much as is needed. And I tell you,

> ask and it will be given you,
> seek and you will find,
> knock and it will be opened to you,

for everyone asking receives, and the one seeking finds, and to the one knocking it will be opened.

Is there of you an abba whose son asking for a fish will hand to him a snake instead of a fish? Or asking for an egg will hand to him a scorpion?

If you, being evil, know to give good gifts to your children, how much more will the heavenly Abba give the **Holy Spirit** to those who ask.

Luke 11:5-13

31 days of the HOLY SPIRIT

1. The SPIRIT WILL REST on HIM — Isaiah 11:1-5
2. The SPIRIT of the LORD — Isaiah 61:1-2a,10-11
3. SPIRIT of the SON of GOD — Galatians 4:3-7 & 5:16,22-23,25
4. The BEGOTTEN of the SPIRIT — Matthew 1:18-25
5. HE WILL BAPTIZE YOU in the SPIRIT — Mark 1:1-8
6. BEHELD the SPIRIT — John 1:29,32-34
7. LED by the SPIRIT into the DESERT — Mark 1:12-13
8. BLASPHEMING against the HOLY SPIRIT — Mark 3:22-30, Matthew 12:24-32, Luke 12:10
9. DAVID and the HOLY SPIRIT — Mark 12:35-37
10. The HOLY SPIRIT SPEAKING — Mark 13:1-11
11. FULL of JOY in the HOLY SPIRIT — Luke 10:17-24
12. HOW MUCH MORE — Luke 11:1-13
13. HE WILL TEACH YOU EVERYTHING — John 14:15-26
14. ASCENSION — Beginning of the Book of Acts 1:1-9
15. From ELEVEN to TWELVE — Acts 1:12-17,21-26
16. PENTECOST — Acts 2:1-4,12-13
17. PETER: WITNESSES — Acts 2:37-39 & 5:30-32
18. STEPHEN, FIRST MARTYR — Acts 7:54-60
19. PHILIP in SAMARIA — Acts 8:5-8,14-20
20. CONVERSION of SAUL — Acts 9:1-9,17-19
21. ANOINTED with the HOLY SPIRIT — Acts 10:37-45
22. FIRST CALLED CHRISTIANS — Acts 11:19-26 & 13:1-4
23. LETTER to the NATIONS — Acts 15:22a,23-29
24. PAUL LAYING HANDS — Acts 19:1-10
25. PAUL to the ELDERS of EPHESUS — Acts 20:22-32
26. PAUL in ROME — End of the Book of Acts 28:25b-31
27. SPIRIT of ADOPTION — Romans 8:14-27
28. JOY in the HOLY SPIRIT — Romans 14:13-19
29. PETER on PROPHECY — 2nd Peter 1:16-21
30. UNITY of the SEVEN ONES — Ephesians 4:3-6
    DO NOT GRIEVE the HOLY SPIRIT — Ephesians 4:25-32
31. By the POWER — Ephesians 3:16-21
    a. Into which ANGELS LONG to LOOK — 1st Peter 1:10-12
    b. The SPIRIT SEARCHES ALL THINGS — 1st Corinth 2:1-16

Bless-ed be the God and Ab-ba
of our Lord/ Je-sus Christ,
Who has blessed us in the Christ\,
bless-ings in their Spir-it breath.
As God chose us in the Mes-si-ah
be-fore/ found-ing sky or earth,
To be ho-ly, clean of blem-ish,
in God's eye: a-dop-tion worth.

In the Son we have re-demp-tion,
God's for-give-ness of our sin,
By the rich-es of his grace\
lav-ished on us gath-ered in.
Giv-ing wis-dom, know-ledge/, vis-ion,
mys-t'ry/ of the Ab-ba's will,
Sum-ming up all things in Je-sus,
fa-vored in the full-ness sent.

In our hear-ing of the gos-pel
word of our sal-va\-tion,
One by one we too were cho-sen,
joined as part-ners with the Son.
By the prom-is'd Ho-ly/ Spir-it,
signed and/ sealed as heirs of God,
God's pos-ses-sion, God's re-demp-tion,
God's be-lov-ed, Ab-ba's own.

Text: **Eph 1:3-14**, Stephen J. Wolf, grateful to the Institute for Priestly Formation, 2008
Music: HYMN TO JOY, Ludwig van Beethoven, d. 1827; adapt. Edward Hodges, 1824
Melody: *Joyful, Joyful, We Adore Thee*

8th
The CHRISTIAN LIFE

readings selected from the
Liturgy of the Hours

Abba Father,
Christ Brother,
Guiding Spirit,
One God in Three Persons,
give us true humility
to see ourselves as you see us

with your gifts to give
through very human weakness,

courageous charity
to not judge others,

and power willing
to do the good

as we seek to love you our God
with heart and mind
and soul and strength

and our neighbors as ourselves.
Amen.

CHRISTIAN LIFE
3
COMFORT - ENCOURAGEMENT

Blessed be the God and Abba
of our Lord Jesus Christ,
Abba of compassion and God of all comfort,
comforting-consoling-encouraging us
in all our affliction
that we may be able
to comfort those in every affliction
through the comfort by which we ourselves
are comforted by God.
As the sufferings of Christ abound in us,
so through Christ also abounds our comfort.
Now when we are afflicted
it is on behalf of your comfort and salvation;
when we are comforted
it is on behalf of your comfort
enduring in the same sufferings
which we also suffer.
Our hope for you is firm
knowing that as you partake in the sufferings
so also you partake of the comfort.

Saint Paul, **2nd Letter to the Corinthians 1:3-7**
The Greek word paraklesis *can mean comfort or consolation or encouragement.*

CHRISTIAN LIFE
13
I AM PERSUADED

Who will separate us from the love of Christ?
Affliction? Distress?
Persecution? Famine?
Nakedness? Peril?
The Sword?
But in all these things we overconquer
through the one who has loved us.
For I am persuaded
that not death
nor life
nor angels
nor rulers
nor present things
nor things coming
nor powers
nor height
nor depth
nor any other creature
will be able to separate us
from the love of God
in Christ Jesus our Lord.

Saint Paul, **Letter to the Romans 8:35,37-39**

31 days on the CHRISTIAN LIFE

1. O the DEPTH — Saint Paul to the Romans 11:30-36
2. CROWD TOO MANY to NUMBER — Saint John in the Book of Revelation 7:9-12
3. COMFORT-ENCOURAGEMENT — Paul in 2nd Corinthians 1:3-7
4. DOING GOOD — Paul, in 2nd Thessalonians 3:7-13
5. PUT ON the LORD JESUS CHRIST — Paul to the Romans 13:11-14
6. CHILDREN of GOD — 1st Letter of Saint John 3:1-3
7. WORD PLANTED in YOU — Letter of Saint James 1:19-27
8. REBIRTH to a LIVING HOPE — 1st Letter of Saint Peter 1:3-9
9. THESE THINGS ABOUNDING — 2nd Letter of Peter 1:3-11
10. GRACE of GOD — Paul to the Colossians 1:3-6
11. CHILDREN of the DAY — Paul in 1st Thessalonians 5:1-11
12. ALL HAVE SINNED — Paul to the Romans 3:21-31
13. I AM PERSUADED — Paul to the Romans 8:35,37-39
14. LIVING and ABIDING WORD of GOD — 1st Ltr of Ptr 1:22-25
15. IF YOUR ENEMY IS HUNGRY — Paul to the Romans 12:9-21
16. GOD IS LOVE — 1st Letter of John 4:15-21
17. MERCY EXULTS over JUDGMENT — James 2:1-13
18. ONE IS the LAWGIVER & JUDGE — James 4:1-12
19. CHARISMS — Paul to the Romans 12:1-8
20. GOOD STEWARDS of GRACE — 1st Letter of Peter 4:7-11
21. SUFFICIENT to YOU IS MY GRACE — 2nd Corinth. 12:1-10
22. To THIS YOU WERE CALLED — 1st Letter of Peter 3:8-11
23. LET ENDURANCE WORK — Letter of James 1:2-11
24. GOD IS the ONE WORKING in YOU — Paul to the Philippians 2:12-16
25. THIS IS MY GOSPEL — Paul in 2nd Timothy 2:1-13
26. For GOOD & for BUILDING UP — Paul to the Romans 15:1-5
27. WALK as HE HIMSELF WALKED — 1st Letter of John 2:1-6
28. PUT ON the NEW HUMAN — Paul to the Colossians 3:5-17
29. BE RECONCILED — Paul to the Colossians 1:21-28
30. CHRIST LIVES in ME — Paul to the Galatians 2:15-21
31. NEW HEAVENS and a NEW EARTH — End of the 2nd Letter of Peter 3:1b-18

Small Ink Brush Drawings: Some years ago a prayer blessing came, a scribbled outline of Charles Dickens' take on the Jesus story written for his children in 1849. Some years later, after a workshop on the calligraphy of Thomas Merton, came the drawings in this book, following Dickens' outline.

But what outline do you use when you tell the story of Jesus?

outline of *THE LIFE OF OUR LORD* by Charles Dickens

Birth of Jesus.
Shepherds of the field and Wise Men of the East.
Murder of the Innocents by Herod the Great.
12-year-old Jesus with the Doctors in the Temple.
Jesus is baptized by John.
Temptation in the Wilderness.
Miracle during the marriage feast at Cana.
Naming of the Twelve.
Great catch of fish.
Teachings on prayer, including the "Our Father."
Healing of a leper, a man with palsy, a servant of
a centurion, and a daughter of a magistrate.
Challenges of the Pharisees.
Raising of the only son of the widow of Nain.
Jesus sleeps in the boat in a storm;
Jesus awakes and stills the storm.
Casting of evil spirits into a herd of swine.
Imprisonment and beheading of John the Baptist.
A woman washes Jesus' feet with her hair.
A man ill for 38 years, at the pool of Bethesda.
Feeding of 5,000 plus, from 5 loaves and 2 fish.
Walking on water and many more healing miracles.
Feeding of 4,000 plus, from 7 loaves and a few fish.
Sending of the Disciples into towns and villages.
Jesus predicts his Death, Rising, and Ascending.
Transfiguration on Mount Tabor.
Jesus cures a mad boy the Disciples could not.
Teachings on being childlike
and forgiving 70 times 7 times.
Stories of the unforgiving steward and a generous master.
Jesus and the accusers of the adulterous woman.

The Greatest Commandment.
Story of the Good Samaritan.
Story of the excuses of those invited to a great supper.
Jesus calls out to Zacchaeus in the tree.
Story of the Prodigal Son.
Story of the Rich Man and Lazarus.
A proud man and a humble man in the Temple.
Jesus is challenged about paying a tax to Caesar.
Example of the widow and her two mites.
Resuscitation of Lazarus of Bethany.
Mary of Bethany anoints Jesus' feet with oil.
Jesus enters Jerusalem on an ass. Hosanna!
Jesus casts out the tables of the money changers.
More of the blind and the lame are healed by him.
Jesus washes the feet of the Disciples.
Jesus says there is one who will betray him.
Judas Iscariot accepts thirty pieces of silver.
The Last Supper.
Jesus predicts that Peter will deny him 3 times.
Jesus prays and the Disciples sleep in Gethsemane.
Judas arrives with a guard and kisses Jesus.
Peter denies Jesus, the cock crows, and Peter weeps.
The Scribes and Priests agree Jesus is to be killed.
Judas throws the silver at the Chief Priests and takes his life.
Chief Priests spend the silver on Potters' Field.
Jesus is questioned by Pontius Pilate.
Pilate has Jesus beaten, mocked, and crowned with thorns.
Pilate says, "Behold the man!" Crowds cry, "Crucify him!"
Pilate washes his hands.
Jesus is nailed alive to a great wooden Cross.
Four soldiers divide Jesus' clothes and gamble over his coat.
People who pass that way mock him.
John the Beloved and four women stay, including Mary.
A deep and terrible darkness comes over the whole land.
A soldier puts to Jesus' mouth a sponge dipped in vinegar.
Jesus says, "It is finished" and "Father, I commend my spirit."
Joseph & Nicodemus wrap & bury the body in a new tomb.
Mary Magdalene sees the rolled away stone.
Peter and John the Beloved go into the empty tomb.
The appearances of the Risen Lord begin.

PASCHAL MYSTERY

1
MANY OTHER THINGS

Jesus does many and other signs
in the presence of the disciples,
which have not been written in this book.
But these have been written
that you may believe
that Jesus is the Christ, the Son of God,
and that believing
you may have life in his name.

John 20:30-31

There are also many other things Jesus does,
which if they were written singly,
I think not the cosmos itself would contain
the bibles being written.

Conclusion of the Gospel of **John 21:25**

www.ingramcontent.com/pod-product-compliance
Lightning Source LLC
Chambersburg PA
CBHW041133110526
44592CB00020B/2791